In the Terrible Weather of Guns

In the Terrible Weather of Guns

John B. Lee

The **Mansfield** Press

National Library of Canada Cataloguing in Publication

Lee, John B., 1951-
    In the Terrible Weather of Guns / John B. Lee

Poems
ISBN 1-894469-10-0
    1. Title
PS8573.E348152 2002   C811'.54   C2002-903904-5
PR9199.3.L39152 2002

The publication of In the Terrible Weather of Guns has been generously
supported by The Canada Council for the Arts and the
Ontario Arts Council.

Cover Design by Gabriel Caira
Text Design by Tim Hanna
Cover Photo by Wonderfile
Author Photo courtesy of Roger Bell

Acknowledgements
Poems from "In the Terrible Weather of Guns" have appeared in, Cranberry Tree Press
Anthology: $10 Cash Value: An Anthology of Assets; Following the Plough: recovering
the rural; Carousel Magazine in which the poem "Martyrs in the Landscape" received
a first honourable mention; Windsor Review in which the poem, "When You Throw
a Man in the Lake," received first honourable mention; The Canadian Poetry
Association Anthology 2002; "The River None Believe," appears on the Niagara Falls
Poetry Project web site; and the essay, "The Life and Times of Joseph Willcocks (1773-
September 4, 1814)" appeared in serialized form in three subsequent issues of
"Family History News."

Mansfield Press Inc.
25 Mansfield Avenue
Toronto, Ontario, Canada
M6J 2A9
www.mansfieldpress.net

Printed in Canada

for the forgotten and the maligned

*with thanks to John Tyndall and Roger Bell
for their editorial assistance*

Contents

On the afternoon of September 4, 1814.../ 11
quotations... / 12

Part the first

Dead Angels Bless Us All / 17
The River Liffey Near Dublin / 19
excerpt from letter to my father, June 7th, 1800 / 21
My Old Wild Ways / 22
excerpt from letter to my brother, November 3, 1800 / 24
The Fever of Stolen Property / 25
excerpts from two letters... / 27
Excellent Reasons to Hate / 28
excerpts from three letters... / 31
Exile / 32

Part the second

Upper-Canadian Oak / 37
What of These Names / 39
excerpts from diaries and letters... / 41
If I Dared to Dream of Father Dying / 42
The Portrait Not Quite There / 44
excerpts from diaries... / 46
Reading Circle / 47
excerpts from diaries and letters / 49
My Heart is Wrung / 50
Writing When the Ink is Cold / 52
excerpt from diary, Sunday, August 6, 1801 / 53
When You Throw a Man in the Lake / 54
excerpts from diaries... / 56

Caught Pulling the Cord Together / 58
excerpts from letter and diaries... / 60
A Disapproval of Stones / 61
Debts / 63
excerpts from diaries and letter / 65
Watching for Wolves / 66

Part the third

excerpts from letters... / 70
The Age of Reason / 71
Hornbook / 72
excerpts from conversations and letters / 74
The Politics of Crows / 75
excerpt from an editorial written by Joseph Willcocks,
       dated June 9, 1812 / 76
Ill Emissary / 77
Gentleman Volunteer / 79
Before the Parliament Was Burned / 82

Part the fourth

Joseph Willcocks' Address to the Disaffected / 87
epithet quoted from the burning of Newark / 89
Burning Home / 90
Treason / 92
The Lie Agreed Upon / 94
A Carnival of Clown's Light Now / 100
"Oh! What are those? What is that?" / 103
Wounded By Bones / 105
From the Opposite Side of the Water / 107

Part the last

The River None Believe / 113
Martyrs in the Landscape / 116
Waterless Children / 118

—notes on the poems—

Notes on the Poems / 121

Afterward: A Matter of Treason—
The Life and Times of Joseph Willcocks
(1773 – September 4, 1814) / 127

On the afternoon of September 4, 1814, Lieutenant-Colonel Joseph Willcocks died from a fatal wound in the right breast suffered in his 41st year. He fell sometime between four and five in the afternoon upon his handsome bachelor's shadow where his green-banded, white-cockaded hat tumbled empty, near the British battery of Lieutenant George Philpotts, located in the woods eight hundred yards outside the earthworks of Fort Erie, Upper Canada. The Americans held the border fort they had not built; that was not theirs to keep. The British lay siege against that shame. Either they had been fighting in close action for six hours, or an accidental encounter with an enemy picket had cost him his soul. Either he had been storming the battery in a blaze of glory, or he had been caught by stray fire in a simple skirmish. By one account, only moments before, Willcocks' intrepid former neighbour from Newark, Peter Schramm, had taken aim knowing full well he could name his target. Having sighted his enemy along the barrel of his musket, he then sent the ball home in a simple motion as with a single puff of awful smoke he brought down his foe in an instant. Or perhaps, as some say, anonymous had set his sights upon a stranger. Thus ended the career of the hot-headed Irish-Canadian traitor. He was silenced. His diaries became ghost works. His letters were orphaned of their author. His journals fixed themselves dead upon the page. His fiery politics muttered into nothing. His desires were rendered morbid; and all his hopes consumed to dust.

When Lieutenant-Colonel Joseph Willcocks expired into that immediate and all-consuming darkness that comes but once, the sky broke open and a rainstorm cooled the ardour of the combatants of both armies. And King Joe breathed no more. To that event the British cheered as to the righteous culmination of a villainy. And the Americans, before he was so famously forgotten, marked his passing with these honoured words, saying, "that in every movement he behaved like a hero and patriot. Calm and unruffled, he rushed on in defense of our country's rights until he fell entwined with the laurels of glory..." And so it went in the War of 1812, after the damned and unprovoked summer invasion. And so it transpired in the second War of Independence, when the Yankees came north in a righteous response to British wrongs.

"Willcocks does not possess a sufficiency of brains to bait a mouse trap."
    Chief Justice Thorpe
    (friend and patron)

"that seditious printer"
    Sir Francis Gore,
    Lieutenant Governor of Upper Canada

"He has all the jealousy of power and all the malignity of rank opposition to struggle with."
    the Reverent Robert Addison, clergy
    Church of England at Newark, July 1, 1807

"Willcocks has become a zealous loyalist. He has behaved very well on all occasions and so have all his party, although they are trusted with no office whatsoever."
    William Hamilton Merritt, February 1813

"Willcocks is surpassed by none in enterprise and bravery."
    the United State Army, 1813

"Calm and unruffled, he rushed on in defense of his country's rights until he fell entwined with laurels of glory..."
    Major A. Matteson,
    United States Army, to General Ripley,
    September 5, 1814

"Joseph Willcocks misfortune was that he was in advance of his Canadian fellow citizens in demanding their rights and determined and uncompromising, like a fearless patriot, in maintaining them."
> extract from the
> "Life and Times of Joseph Willcocks"
> taken from "Irish Celts,"
> Detroit, 1884

"Willcocks was a tonguey, tricky, unscrupulous, bad-living fellow."
> William Kirby,
> poet and amateur historian,
> Annals of Niagara, 1894

"Plainly, Willcocks was a gentleman, well-educated, intelligent, truthful, capable, courageous."
> Editor's Preface, "The Diary of Joseph Willcocks,
> December 1, 1799-February 1, 1803", 1936

1773 – 1799
Ireland

—part the first—

In which Joseph is born, the second son of Anglo-Irish gentle-folk, Robert Willcocks and Jane Willcocks (nee Powell) at "The Mills" Palmerston, on the River Liffey four kilometers west of Dublin. Following the devastation of the 1798 Irish Rebellion and the near financial ruin of his father, the debt-plagued swain departs for Upper Canada to seek his fortune drawn there with a promise of property and position to be provided by his cousin William.

Dead Angels Bless Us All

If you are born a gentleman
in an age of common rogues
falling from your mother
through the slow gravity
of her birthing bed
born to swim the sharp light
of a wet world
a boy kite
trailing his umbilicus
into that painful brilliance
or a guttering glow of indoor evening
altared and so suddenly chromatic
and so newly limned
it seems to dream itself alive
beyond the water
in the eye
in the open and saltless sea
blue as a second sky.

But if you are born
a gentleman in an age of common rogues
following an elder better son
landless into the world
what then for you
upon those waves of time
your father's house in grave decline
a doldrum in the sails
dead angels still their flight
and with a thoughtless wonder
sink like shrouded gulls
who lift their water-heavy wings
because they drown

and think to fly the deep
inventing heaven as they go
one breathless pause
and then we gasp to sing.

The River Liffey Near Dublin

The River Liffey
exits into its black bay
where bog water makes dark music
for the ghosts of Vikings
and the Norse
and the Norman
and the round-hat wars
with the English God
gone pale as snow at night
falling among these Roman voices
flowing through
a thousand Irish hills
where the Shannon blends
her man-made flux and urge to float
us, and as a boy
I fished these banks for bass
while reed winds whistled
down the dogs
to where the green mind of the land thought of itself
beneath peat-smeared streets
and curs come on as well
to scrap in alleys
remembering their ancient pact
with Joyce unborn
and Yeats not yet conceived
though Swift and Goldsmith
worked an old romance
and sometimes loved the poor
and if I felt the pull
beneath the flow
or saw the sky go past
in brief remorse

to draw my face along
the leaving light
and if I leaned
above my bending rod
my heart set free and wild alive
as dying fish will gasp and gasping dream of water
spilling on their gills

why then the politics of nothing
powers me
and I become a violent absence
an observance of wind in the whispering dead
as death for death
we shape ourselves around
an empty house
that is not there
and howl
a saying wall
where windows hang
like paintings soaked in weather
rocked open
to reveal dark shadows
squared into a lightless
sky.

"I still retain all the boyish tricks I had at home. I have a canoe, a fishing rod and in fact all the sports my mind can wish . . ."

Joseph Willcocks, letter to my dear father,
dated at York, U.C., June 7, 1800

My Old Wild Ways

When I was a boy
I loved the wild ways
to run the Liffey rushes
with my rod
and my flung line
of dark water
to feel the soft pull
of the flow
where fishes thought
as fishes will of silver things
and all along
the dog's joy of a green morning
among horses
in the sun-slow hills
where even time wishes it were still
and I floated
a lad's punt, my own oars
good deep and strong in the locks
as I circle myself
in a gyre
making a rill like rucked black silk
and I dove and swam
in the cold traces
my vanishing heels blinked blind
to chase the silkies of dream
down where they dwell
in the sunken stone
and I took my oak-stocked gun
and my pistol brace to the woods
around and felt the rain-veiled day
chilled and vague of its hour
sun-grey as a road mark stone

in a ten-mile sky, away and away
as if I were proud of my oxblood boots
why then who could blame
me walking under a shadow's weight

who in a turn of wing
that stains the ground greener where it falls
could say
there was no flight of things
and who
in the love of a boy for himself
could deny his wealth
and send him out
from want
with the apple's mass of his human heart
and see him enter then
as they all did then
again and again and a loss
at last alas
into the terrible thrill
of war.

"know beauty will not make the pot boil, which consideration above prevents me from assuming an air of seriousness—Love and runaway matches I never was an advocate for, such proceeding may fill the belly of women, but not of men."

Joseph Willcocks, letter to my brother Richard,
dated at York, U.C., November 3, 1800

The Fever of Stolen Property

these 18th century women
place their beauty spots
as messages
then go to cards.
At whist
the kissing mark
invites a gentle buss
beside the rose-bow
of a painted mouth
to thrill the feminary
with a tiny throb of life
like creatures of the sea
who stir a little milky water
when they wave to move
and this to flirt with fire
in a secret lover's mind
or tease the cuckold husband
so he rush to pistols
in a cordite fog at dawn
and make a ghost of rivals
bleeding on the green
the seconds weeping at the loss of life upon a dew
these men of honour
angry as they die
or then the forehead blemish
tells the fever of stolen property
the fickle coitus
where she loose her longest limbs.

And if that mischief
make the white flesh bloom
like pink light on a lily
or if the lady
set her cap on lying down
as gently as she does
the queen of hearts
upon a bright design
a single powerful suit she wins herself
beneath the jack of knaves
ah Casanova's at the window
like the painter's ladder leaning in
to sweep a little colour on the ledge
meanwhile the closet's crowded
and two bachelors bump
below the bed
how make a moral then
from time's desire
from this comedy of passion
from this age or reason
blown to dust.

.

"...the late unfortunate melancholy rebellion which pervaded our distracted country."

Joseph Willcocks, letter
dated at York, U.C., 1800

"were he (the Lieutenant Governor) acquainted with all my services during the late Irish Rebellion, but we loyal folks sometimes go unrewarded."

Joseph Willcocks, letter to my brother Richard,
dated at York, U.C., April 1802

Excellent Reasons to Hate

Joseph Willcocks and the Irish Rebellion of 1798

We wait in the boredom and terror
of our separate houses
watching the small domestic fires
in our close hearths
and hearing rumours
from Wexford, rumours
from Kildare, women and old men
piked on the road
flown in the air pierced through
the lungs and the loins
how on makeshift gallows
men were hanged or half hanged by the loose half hitch
or marched from their towns
were shot at Dunlavin
or pitch-capped and burned
by a brown-bag crown of powder and tar
murdered in bed
their homes gutted and set
to the torch
hacked to death in their fields
shot while they worked
how 200 souls at Scullabogue barn
were piked and then burned
how at Three Rocks
Fawset's men were engulfed
and scoured from the world
look to the tip of a long lance
how a young girl
pierced through the womb like a doll on a pin
flies in the air

and we heard these things
at the tedium of tea and cakes
in the ennui of evening
with the sun in the west
on the Bay
like the slowing of light
when the brazier dims into ash gone red
and then grey
and we wait
in the violent dark
in the guttering down of a dream
we wake
in the lawless light of the day
when the sun hit the wall
of the world
like a blast from the cannon of God
breaching a hole in the blue *let there be light* of the sky
with the war coming close
and my brother
thrown from the bridge
with half of our hopes
turned under the green flag of the ground
and the bodies at Ballynahinch
lay in the street for the hogs
and rebels blown
from the mouth of a great gun
like chaff gone red
and we in our good rooms
waiting for word
three weeks on the wind
the people, the mob, the rabble,
the deluded masses

their hospital burned at Eniscorthy, wounded
rebels and all
after that the crush of Vinegar Hill
their leaders hanged
with 30,000 dead since early May
with the French boats landed at Mayo
betrayed by Bonaparte
and Napper Tandy drunk at sea
at the end of the golden summer

in the fall when Wolfe Tone
cut his own throat
and stole his own breath
with a swipe of the razor in jail
and we wonder
what bad government will bring
with the ghosts of our time
like smoke
from the feet of dead troops on the march

and what of the loyal
and what of the true
when the land
is all sorrowed with stone
and what is our duty
and who to believe
in this *Erin go Bray*
with our excellent reasons to hate.

"*my Native Country for Government were very dilatory in promoting my interests.*"

Joseph Willcocks, letter,
dated at York, U.C., June 10, 1800

"*I am a most distressed person, and if Providence had not thrown Mr. Russell in my way I am sure I don't know what should become of me.*"

Joseph Willcocks, letter to my father,
dated at York, U.C., September 1, 1800

"*...reflecting on the diminution of my poor Father's property, and how indispensibly necessary it was for me to look out for something for myself and not for my necessary expenses to be an encumbrance upon the little which providence secured for him (my father).*"

Joseph Willcocks, letter to my brother, Richard,
dated at York, U.C., September 1800

Exile

You need not be homeless
to feel without a home
arriving over the great wide blue
amnesia of an angry ocean
forgetful of your life
though memory grieves
to know the dreamer gone away
like someone drowning in the deep wet darkness
of the night

and if you were lost
as you say—
the fateless second son
you've become
and hopeless at home
though you are landless here at first
in Upper Canada cutting the snow
from Albany in the hard winter
the year you came to York the century turning
chased by rumours of war
in Eire and Europe and in America as well
a pitiful creature
a wild young Irish rogue
doomed by what wished you away
into this career of sorrows—
that first winter many lost their hands
your dear father died
your sister went strange
your brother betrayed his trust
your cousin here fell short of his brag
your cousin's son
a duelist

challenged you while you slept
beneath a loaded brace above your bed
and watched the door latch snick
like lost wind and the wolf

how then might history
have known you
in your gentle breeches
and riding boots
learning by the ennui of weather
and the tedium of early dusks
at cards and evening readings
by your sonorous cousin
ill almost to death
and never a letter from home but one
giving the news of how you were orphaned
by an unknown sorrow
addressing your dead father
with epistles
posthumous to his demise.

And ever exiled
ever after Liffey-less
and beholden to the grace
of ghosts and strangers.

1800 – 1806

Arrival at York, UC... and after

—part the second—

In which young Willcocks' fortunes rise and fall at the whim of his patrons. Shortly after his arrival in Upper Canada, Joseph accepts a position as the personal secretary of Peter Russell, the most powerful man then residing in the capital.

He learns of the death of his father in Ireland and, wrongly accused of disloyalty to the crown during the Rebellion of 1798, he suffers his brother Richard's refusal to take his part at home or abroad.

After acquiring land and paying off his debts at home, he falls out of grace with Russell by presuming above his station and courting Russell's sister, Elizabeth.

He makes copies of all his correspondence during this period and keeps a diary of his daily activities beginning with his arrival and ending in February 1803.

Through subsequent attachments, he becomes sheriff of the Home District. However, as the result of personal acquaintance with political radicals and alienation of appointed officials such as the Lieutenant Governor, he falls out of favour and loses his position.

Upper-Canadian Oak

They say two hundred years ago
the oak were tall enough to touch
above the light
an ancient wisdom in the wood
five hundred summers old
and a two-chain girth
in the long-lost rains
of the past before the past
in the axe and wedge and stump-rot
of arriving Europe
when the language of the land
was wind-simple
and thrilled with weed.

I will not hearken back
to when the wolves
romanced the hills of night
without response
as if the lonely moon
were lonelier for that
primordial ulul-arum of the beast.

But what is lost
by ghosts is lost by all
and to know
the nameless rivers knew their names
in the dream-nation of themselves
where water laughs
to lap the shallow rocks
and suck the surface down
in the foamy lashing
of a phantom sky

which never happens twice
and never happens there
unless the water deepens on its own.

And if by dying well
we are to do some good
as it is with
dying into someone else's memory:
a slow forgetting—
the welter of weather
on a stone transformed
until it is no longer stone
—*a making way*

a soul looks down
and loves the child
who holds the past within his heart
six-thousand-year-old cities
rise and fall
within the fertile crescent
of an unborn womb
and like a velvet clock
the silken circle
receives the dreaming seed.

What of These Names

Of Russell, White and Small
Jarvis, Osgoode, McDonnell
Dickson, Addison, Boulton
Merritt, Secord
and Willcocks as well
these Canadian names
transplanted as the century turned
some from their good new homes at Newark/Niagara
and their chain-wide streets
their six-slave houses
and jealous *ladies man* duels
with smoke in a coat
where death's wormed in
and the ticklish politics of the times
when a man
might fall from another's pocket
like a pyx or snuff or watch fobbed loose
or if you follow the power
along the wrong fuse
you die in the burn
of a tallowless wick
of a lamp's black blink
and a stink of brief light
smudged blind and dark in its glass
thumbed clean
where the young soul's soiled
and the heart, corroded by blood
where it snoops the cut
and hurt
of some consanguine hope
too deep to heal
corrupted by the little envies

that we sometimes feel
and if a life is over, looking back
to be measured in gold
surveyed by links of land
and all the hod's-heavy heights
that comfort
the dozenth room
these disappearing doors of air
the widow's lonely years
the weeping seasons
gay summers and slow winters at candle-lit cards
and sonorous books
and if we law the wolves away
why then, they whelp on wind
in little swirls of dust
like walking ghosts with names we speak alive.

"Dreamed that my father was going to be married."

Joseph Willcocks, diary entry,
dated Monday, December 15, 1800

"...a letter from Richard which told me of my father's death on the 1st of March (1800)."

Joseph Willcocks, diary entry,
dated Sunday, January 11, 1801

"Put on mourning for my father."

Joseph Willcocks, diary entry,
dated Sunday, January 18, 1801

"...for three weeks back I mourned for my father as if I knew he had been dead, my dreams were the strongest and most expressive that had ever floated on the imagination in so much that I had a PRESENTMENT *of his death."*

Joseph Willcocks, letter to my brother Richard,
dated at York, U.C. January 18, 1801

If I Dared to Dream
of Father Dying

the ocean
is such slow news
the nights a long
and moon-drowned darkness there.
I slept away sad letters.
Spent epistolary hours
writing hopes of home
and him dead
these many months since then
reading the stars beneath him
and everything else
aging into dust
my pen flies, unwitting
among sorrows, orphaned
by earth
and its leaning stones.
If I dared to dream him dead
in prescient sleep
if he came to me with feathered shoes
if he were but a lantern
full of light
his skull a gourd and candle
I might not weep to wake
and see no more—
I might hold as irony
the little tricks of God
whose deep wide waters
make a jest of time
and all anachronism
of the present clock.
Oh brother, such a loss

to think of father dead
to know I wrote
a living line
that sank into the page
like light in brackish swells
for one who owned his name no more
if I dared to dream of father dying
then of these foolish
letters to a ghost
make nothing but a want of news.
I am a child of stale design.

The Portrait Not Quite There

Yours is the portrait not quite there among those dour and corpulent cousins who hang on the brush with lidded eyes dripped open wet and mouths heavy with paint as red as indoor roses. Yours is the wall shadow where in a slightly bright perimeter the hue is clean and clear as the shape of a window shining in a ghost-framed light.

Your wealthy cousins sat in the artist's eye like portly candles tallowing down in the mind when the mind no longer sees. And if he stroke the canvas twice to brush the throat where it wattles in the collar, or if he cock a tuft of hair come ruffling where the scalp yields something weed wild tempting to be greened another day and from baroque and ugly gold gild wood his hands almost lean out as on a sash to call the children home and the white well-leavened ten-mooned two drain from the cuff like cream poured slow to tip a manicure...

But yours is tomorrow's work. The artist whittles his leads to the nub. Blacks his thumb on night. Smears an inner oil and stirs his colours in a swirl the canvas cannot catch. How like a changing sky the mutable firmament of seasons and storms above water. How like the deeps and shallows of light where we might trail a disappearing touch upon the liquid glass that shows our faces flowing on the twilit glaze where a lamp betrays the dark leaving this window's wonder with us: are we ourselves?

And you whose face has drowned in clay, your eyes brushed over with dust as we all must enter the dead-dog darkness of dusk so hard to see surrounded and eternally blinded to the close at hand in the far away. And there you are two-hundred autumns since you fell to winter in the land. And if I hang an empty canvas in the wind to catch the rain, the water marks the weather in a yellow stain. How long until it rag into a handsome vision where you were? How long until the heavens tear blue silk upon the driven nail?

"Mr. Russell read of Portrait of Elvira..."

"Mr. Russell finished vol. of Joseph Andrews.."

"Mr. Russell read The History of the Bible..."

"Mr. Russell read first vol. Peregrine Pickle..."

"Mr. Russell read part of Tom Jones..."

"Mr. Russell read from Gulliver's Travels..."

"Mr. Russell read Lord Chatham's speeches against the American War..."

"Mr. Russell read the History of Henry VIII for us..."

"Mr. Russell read part of Charles the 1st for us..."

"...they saw that I was drunk..."

Joseph Willcocks, various diary entries
dated between November 15, 1800
and March 19, 1802

"There is such a never ceasing sameness here..."

Joseph Willcocks, letter to my brother Richard,
dated at York, U.C., April 1802

Reading Circle

Winter evenings spent in candle glow
the women blushing red
by the fire-screen embroidery
that shields their flickering faces from desire
while Peter Russell
the old rock reads
with sonorous voice
stentorian and droning
in the sleepy light where shadows flew
like bird-winged ghosts
on the white-washed walls
and we heard
of Gulliver roped to a Lilliputian shore
those little men
like voles with strings
had trapped him down, poor lad like me...
still later the Yahoo horses yawped—
and then we laughed
at the brumous farts of science
when the fire flared in the hearth
as if from sulfur's help
and the noisome health of the well-fed
gouty fellow close at hand
and ah, the tired logs rolled down and sagged
like wine-drunk rogues in bed
and the brazier drifted ash
to a cold-grey smoky snowing off of time
and the Bible voices
vicared by the moralizing overlay
of pages
with all the ennui
of soporific snoring

to content our souls.
But I for one
would watch the rosy coin
burn forth
from inner embers of desire
in the flesh which spent and vanished
brief as petal water stains
a breathing thought
and in that redolent interval
of being watched
tiny flowers fevered up
within the frail relaxing open in the honey-brilliant flame
and when the book's clapped shut
with a clup and the blind ink's
kissed the dark completely
old Peter's rocked his skull
like Christ's last stone to seal his secret tomb
and we've all gone our way
and I am in my room alone
under a dreamer's fist of stars
I'd wonder
where the lonely women were
and what they did
and why within our mutual solitudes
we'd married such a dark
like a black cloth folded twice
along an emptiness.

"your friend Weekes is entirely out with all parties and I believe out with all very poor."

Joseph Willcocks, letter
dated at York, U.C., June 6, 1802

"Mr. John McKay brought over word from Niagara that Weekes was there mad."

Joseph Willcocks, diary entry,
Wednesday, September 15, 1802

My Heart is Wrung

In a dream
I see the dreary muzzle smoke
withering off the duel
of the gun's exhale
heavy with the loss of life
for our friend, poor Weekes, who fell this day
the hole in his coat . . . the brilliant red
of a fatal boutonniere
bored where the slug has split his ribs
to find his fatal heart
and burn
a surgeon's brand for valentine
so finger-sized the soul leaked out
as easy
as a winter chimney
where the dizzy birds fall in the flue
and all the wide
accepting sky
mere wool-tags of our going
each wolf-toothed star
enough of light to hang a death upon
the appetite of dogs
and if I weep to ask you all
"does he yet blaze?
  and his mortal anger gone
  as rage sufficient
  in that effrontery of little men
  who mark a wrong
  I saw him stand his distance
  statue still as with the courage of the mad
  he held his heavy and unnatural arm
  until the feckless spat

of human flesh
  learned otherwise and laid him flat"
I saw him carried from the field
I saw him set aside
I heard him sundered, grieved and sobbed about
I felt him sink
in the hard swallow of my sorrow
like apple ache
and the cruel burn
so suddenly vague with stupid sleep we are
made double heavy with our
better loves and worser hates.

Writing When the Ink is Cold

I've been writing late
when the ink is cold
with the slow black drag
of the quill
and the candle guttering down
on the hiss of its wick
and the shadows
drawing their dark
in the less than dark
which is darker for them
where they wave in the tallow melt of time
and tomorrow
this will remain
this looping that follows the hand
in this small unremembering room
all alone—and was I thinking of home
or was I thinking of here
with the past on the page.

And then like fat wax
at the seal of the dawn
flowing east after sleep
the sun rises red in the blue
as these peregrinations from the day before
grow dry
as rainless loam
and I remember the wind.

"I threw young Hale into the lake for untying my boat."

Joseph Willcocks, diary entry,
Sunday, August 6, 1801

When You Throw a Man in the Lake

I saw my good little boat
had left its slip
then floated away
so lovely and light
it was where it went to be gone
like a fallen leaf in the lake
from empty oar locks
and closed up sail
to the shallow wake of an empty thing
like the shadow drag
of a linden tree's shade
and it was lost to me and briefly free
to set its own charts to the will of tide
where the rock of waves
might make a lonesome lover
of its hollow hull
and it might navigate
the fathoms of some buried stone
where it bumps and draws itself
like a caught saw
without a scar in the wood save the wet draft
of its plimsol line
to worry away
by the half-wind west and out
along a doze of dark-drowned towns.

And if I blame
the captain's fog
and if he settle for a sundial wet with mist
with a moony nimbus
for an astrolabe
or if he set his course by the wheeling stars

of campfire sparks
and aim his long blind glass
at the lie of land
with no eye to the way
of this
why then—do not ask—
why a fellow might feel
that justice is there for him
if he throw a man in the lake
for his careless knots.

Can you feel the whiskey barrel
of his girth in your arms
at the end of the dock
where you send him
flying in like a fluttering boy—
say—learn your half hitch now!!—
there's a hangman's noose
on the midnight moon
and the lake is pulling the light.

"...spoke a little funny to a certain person on a certain subject..."

Joseph Willcocks, diary entry,
Wednesday, October 13, 1800

"I stayed most of the day with Miss Russell."

Joseph Willcocks, diary entry,
Saturday, December 6, 1800

"I was a little huff with Miss Elizabeth Russell."

Joseph Willcocks, diary entry,
Monday, December 8, 1800

"I stayed late the whole day with the ladies."

Joseph Willcocks, diary entry,
Thursday, February 19, 1800

"Miss Russell was in the sulks."

Joseph Willcocks, diary entry,
Monday, March 23, 1801

"Wrote a letter to Miss Russell and she sent it back."

Joseph Willcocks, diary entry,
August 6, 1801

"Miss Russell mended my sails."

Joseph Willcocks, diary entry,
Monday, August 7, 1801

"Miss Russell and I were alone and dined on Beef and Veal. Spoke sharply to her on her promise."

Joseph Willcocks, diary entry,
Monday, December 21, 1801

"I returned to Miss Russell every article I had of hers and paid her 21 dollars."

Joseph Willcocks, diary entry,
Wednesday, December 23, 1801

Caught Pulling the Cord Together

And if not for my heart's hope lost
my dear Elizabeth, I'd never think of you
though we saw the falls true weight gone white
when it was grass and thunder
from the water's roar
a beast of mist and green stone
that slipped the edge of everything
and if I had not held
your dainty hand
and watched you step the difficult rim
of the world
and float five-bannered light
through fairy's weather
where the sun was cooled and combed
of colour
in an arc that rose
like an angel thinking of itself elsewhere
and if we
had not picnicked on the table rock
cold salmon melting
on our appetites and claret washed
or seen the monarchs
chase themselves away
like autumn leaves
bent double on a fold of vein
with all the vanity
of summer to regret
or seen them light and lift away
as easy as a memory perfumed

and if we had not
cut through snow
the quick-belled horses
breathing hard as if they burned
long faces in the wind
and you were laughing
muffled and rug-wrapped
as we went
and though we sat
where clock hands worked
black circles like an ox-shaft milling grist
the shorter washing the well-shadow of the first
and so were caught at cards
bussing in the heat of the hearth
your bachelor brother hating that
and you fled blushing
like something rubbed too hard
and if not then for my heart's lost hope
your love's as fickle as a water stain
and I'm forgot...

"All the American ladies (at least those which I have seen) are either too forward or too ugly for me to form a matrimonial connection with."

Joseph Willcocks, letter to my brother Richard, dated at York, U.C., April 1802

"Went with Sutherland the Mason to examine Stones on Adjutant McGill's Farm. We did not approve of them."

Joseph Willcocks, diary entry, Thursday, February 1, 1803

A Disapproval of Stones

Somewhere between a gentleman and his land
there is a broken bargain
from a war of weeds on the wind like a blown-black sea
to the root work
thick in the ground
like the suddenly real shadow of branches
sunk down
for a clutch to the shock of the axe
a hold-steady claw
though you rock at a stump
like a rotten tooth in the jaw
of the skull of the world, it stays
and then
there's the lack of the heaving of stone
the scatter up thaw
you must drag to the ditches
or off to the building of barns
and there like the grit of a groan
they float from the earth
appear like the bulge of a gouty old fact
lying down to take rest
on the clay
a solid settle of unbuttoned uncles
unbuckled by fallow
and the flaws of late frost.
And if by God's disapproval of stones
I am not cursed, why then I'm cursed
by their rumble and clack and their
pinching of hands
the fumbled-off weight
of things found
lifted where the gravity's more lazy

but the wind is weak
though it flex its cruel weather
like a common clock
in the counting house of over-heavy time.

Debts

The first man I saw
hanged in Canada was Irish
strangled as he dropped through the squared floor
under a clay-coloured winter sky
of muddy-winded morning, scaffolded
with the last dry leaves
rattling like ghosts
in filthy tatters
and he, a counterfeit
among the fat well-healed shills
the shop-keep greedy Scots
and I think
of all the pounds I owe
from more golden days of Dublin
at home on the Liffey shore
where I once lived
how I came coining once mere ounces
in my mother's womb
the sperm-split ovum
startled to be spent
and good father milk-poor for that
and less landed
in a borrowing age
when the young are ruined
by the too-deep draft of life
as dram by dram
I drank the claret dry
and from my breeches and boots
lent a gentleman's airs
to the tailor's trust
and the cobbler's nail
and the cane-maker's monogram

made from the silver scrimshaw of a jeweler's scratch
J.W., I am out of hope
and by a crooked neck
reminded of raynard's leap and the howl of the bloody hound
with the grey breath of my cantering horse
and the pistol brace
loaded from above a worried bed
how moneyed men control the earth
and by the burning coin of day
or the pale guilt of the gilded moon
manage a poor forgery of home
made to warn the warming world
from cold sterling and the cool commerce of eternal night.

"Sat up at the Farm all last Night Watching for the Wolf."

Joseph Willcocks, diary entry,
Wednesday, September 23, 1801

"There was great depredations committed the night before last by a flock of wolves that came into the town."

Joseph Willcocks, letter to my brother Richard,
dated at York, U.C., November 3, 1800

Watching for Wolves

I am watching for wolves.
And the night
surrounds us
as each hour whelps a star
in a loupe of time
and the winter
howls in the float holes
of the barn barely built
and the sheds half there
and dies in the voice of trees
at rough horizon's edge
where the ulularum
of the pack
mourns the otherwise empty dark.
If the moon pull
terror on a sled of light
and water unwomb from the deep
and climb the land
where stones on the lip of the lake
slake a shattered white
I wait
locked in the fear of sheep
under a gutted storm
its guttural rumble rolling
in a fleece of weather
shorn of snow
and though I law the world
in a lunar month
the wolf bitch leaps
in a loom of light
and fades to smoke
in a red-mouthed dawn

and where she was
sad-fated quiet comes
and where she goes
in the jointed white
where land meets land
and lambs away
in a long look
a mystery material
to walking a map
of parchment with a pen
to where we go
from whence we came
in the gut of the wolf
a cathedral of ribs bent round for stars.

1807 — July 1813

the Newark years
and the coming of war

—part the third—

In which Willcocks leaves Upper Canada and then returns to take up residence at Newark where he establishes "The Upper Canadian Guardian or Freeman's Journal," the first political newspaper to appear in the province. Willcocks is three times elected to the Legislature, the first being in 1808 representing the riding of West York, Lincoln and Haldimand.

A political populist and bombastic journalist, he finds himself charged and jailed for sedition.

With the coming of war in June 1812, Willcocks spends his last loyal year, first serving General Brock as a successful emissary to the Grand River Natives, then fighting with courage and distinction as a gentleman volunteer at the Battle of Queenston Heights, and finally writing pro-British documents encouraging enrollment in the local militia before going over to the other side at Fort George in July 1813.

"...as I have always been too insignificant a Being to take part in a Political Question. I have no ambition and assume now that which I always disliked and to which I have no title or sentence. But let the question be carried or not carried, it shall never warp my affections from the existing government of England."

Joseph Willcocks, letter
dated at York, U.C., 1800

"The government have seen to place great confidence in my loyalty which confidence I assure you shall never be broken by any act of mine."

Joseph Willcocks, letter
dated at York, U.C., September 1,
1800

"I see how peace is to benefit us."

Joseph Willcocks, letter
dated at York, U.C., June 6, 1802

The Age of Reason

It was *the age of reason*
and these were *the rights of man*
the revolutionary spirit free and wild
in America, in France, in Ireland—
old Tory worries plagued the poor
and parliament and King's concern were set
confluent with wars of faith
when most ideas took up guns
intemperate words and drunken saws
and where the power was like shifting dark
when dark was barely there...
and who was in or out or up or down
from when the ice
like whimsey glass
might weigh the winter woods
and make a cane of shine and be
fool's beauty of a season
ruined by a brilliant light
to when the summer streams
ran rooking all the green the same as now.
And if by thought we're known
the zeitgeist then was *war*
and nations shifting colours
like the crawl of flame.

Hornbook

I have in the hornbook of my youth
written certain things
about myself
no longer true—
so what!
I have set down
in diaries
such violence and joy
aspiring in the thumb drag
of wet letters
and been blue handed as the dead
for all of that,
I'm an amanuensis, echoing my kind
for such kings as there were, such countries
such lady liars
such fickle men...
it changed my blood
one vowel counted
at each pulse point
jumping like a pecking egg.

Inconstant consonants
I am owed wings
where all my hopes took flight.

By diatribes and dithyrambs
I shake my coat to breathe
and blot
a better purpose
from the well
my fellow man
I slap the child I was

awake to walk the grassy way
between two fields
that balk beneath his boots
and shift him up and down like water crests
for he must work
the brawling ground
to be the man I am become.

"I am most shamefully and most cruelly oppressed for reasons unknown to myself . . . and cannot say a word in vindication."

Joseph Willcocks in conversation,
November 27, 1806

"By God, the country from repeated infringements upon rights and liberties, is now ripe for anything."

Joseph Willcocks in conversation,
November 27, 1806

"When they are properly stated at home, and when we shall have made some other arrangements in the government, we shall carry all before us, by God."

Joseph Willcocks in conversation,
November 27, 1806

"In Consequence of General Brock's commands communicated to me thro' you, relative to the Indians upon the Grand River, I made no delay in going among them."

Joseph Willcocks, letter to John Macdonell,
September 1, 1812

The Politics of Crows

I've heard them voting in the trees
by thirty black caws
cacophonies in vocables of hawking wind
singing "where will we go for the good grain"
and what of all
the eagle perils, I'm
in the high pine wag, perched there
a single black-feathered muse
lashing the green sky
like the tail of a great beast
to down through the branches
as weathered fruit
refusing to fall
might hang on past its season
or cling to its inner pit
like the stone-bellied dead.
I have listened
to murders in chorus
coughing an ill song
in a sick dyspepsia of turbulent heavens
I have
in the echo fade
of a lake-wash sky
marked one journeying
out of the cloud-swaddled sun
away from time
and the tyranny of clocks
his jet still clear in turgid detergent of rain
and the sound of his will
set deep beyond the resonant bone
of my own knowing...

"To the Public

...I will yet confound my enemies...

Fellow subjects, this is the last impression the Old Press will make for your benefit while in my possession, it is now about to pass into hands I fear polluted, yet may it be the instrument of good in the hands of evil doers . . . (The Freeman's Journal has been)...a public newspaper, avowedly calculated to disseminate the principles of political truth, check the progress of inordinate power, and keep alive the sacred flame of a just and radical liberty."

J. Willcocks, Editor"

Joseph Willcocks, final editorial,
The Guardian Extra, June 9, 1812

III Emissary

Tell my enemies "Brock came to me!
Not to the villain, Indian agent Claus..."

Perhaps it was but politics
which brought him here to sup
and honour with a humble wish
a man he knew
as popular among the throng
and rabble
or better still
that I and my *cabal*
were known among the Natives on the Grand
as noble and trusted friends.

What that I was ill
and yet I went
what that I was weak
and feckless with a fever
and yet I went
what that I was cramped
and by a bowel's agony
bent double in my tent
and yet I went
what that I suffered
and was sick for weeks
and yet I went
what that I was hated
by the Tory runts
the land-grab leaders
the bribed and bribing few
and yet I went
and so

I hear that history remarks
it must have been another man
how could it have been me

or they say
Brock was deluded, or distracted
mistaken, confused, wrong!
but by the complicated context
of our better selves
I lay claim to this...*the doing of the thing*
for if we rise and fall
as rhythms of a troubled sea
though down
in the death-calm deeps
we find calm darkness
and a heave of heavy light
yet we say
the surface roils
as empty as a drowned man's boat
but we are both at once
the surface and its fathoms too
for we are most ourselves
beyond the brief reflections
where eternal dark resides and no light lies

and yet I went, and yet I went
and yet
                    I went.

Gentleman Volunteer

Joseph Willcocks at the Battle of Queenston Heights

Sheaffe woke us and we rode
or walked
against the flow
a human river out of step with natural time
or widdershins with water winding back the hour
and the sun
we were approaching our own death
as man by man we thought
as if the cattle dust
beneath our morning tramp
were but a trampling up of souls.
How man *in the gorge* were we...
and I upon my mount
imaginary statue on a plinth of land
the limestone generations
heavy in the press of ages
and if we feared to die
above the river roar
if we feared primordial things
in that the last
and less than gentle night
we heard
the crack of distant guns
like sticks that snap in storm
we heard the cloud-burst cannon
and felt the shock and after-shock
that shakes the breathing ribs both ways
and makes the heart
an apple in a wind-wrecked tree.
We but arrived
and all the chaos

of a general death
shivered up the heights
as if in the gathering back
of a caught and broken chain a link were snagged
upon a root
and then we stood our ground

and then we made
each musket volley count
and took revenge
and saw the enemy spill
their courage
like a stone that wrecks its path
upon a hill
and dozens drowned for home
as sheep ticks will
that cannot hold their life
and float a fatal memory
of what they were
mere soldiers
of a lost belief
they tumbled back
and then the day was ours.

And if by one regret I'm known
I'm known by this
that I was blind to how the war of little men
is not the same for large.
How like a toy I was
who felt the hand of God
reach down
to set aright a few

and I'm but made of tin
and painted
like a rust-wet nail
and sent away
to click a cricket song
while others
hold the proud attention
of the wheel of the world
and remain companions
to their shadows in the sun and stone.

Before the Parliament Was Burned

Before the parliament was burned at York
the two long low
buildings served also
as Sunday worship
and the minister sermonizing
on the fear of death
and we sat in our youth
in makeshift pews
under the moralizing drone
of winter
rehearsing an old voice
of cold weather
concerning snow and the wheel of stars.

Before the parliament was burned at York
we sat
in the circle of streams
debating the stumps in the street
and the moonlit howl of the wild
night with malarial fens
sulfurous with frog song
grieving our drowned sons
and frozen fathers
and fearing the day-dark tangle
beyond the roads
with their nettings of shade
and bogged in the mud
or sculpted by frost.

Before the parliament was burned at York
we quarreled in quorums
settled into fractions of men

squabbled over mind and blood
over book and bread
and what we were born to
in the rabbling out of our office.

Before the parliament was burned at York
before the coming of war
when the garrison lamps
lit maps
in a lambent halo of borders
beyond the lake
and the swampy sands
surely then our fortunes and our futures
smouldered away
soul by soul
like the shadows of old women walking.

July 1813 – September 4, 1814

Traitor Willcocks wreathed in laurels

—part the fourth—

In which Joseph abandons Canada, crossing over at Fort George and offering his services to the invading Americans. As a Major elected by the troops, he raises a force of expatriate Canadians calling themselves The Canadian Volunteers.

In his capacity as ranking officer of the Canadian Volunteers he leads a burning party torching his home town of Newark in the winter of 1813, afterwards following the retreating American Army back across the border.

Now a Lieutenant Colonel, Willcocks journeys to Washington for an audience with Secretary of War, John Armstrong. Returning to active duty in May of 1814, he and his Canadian Volunteers engage in raids along the Niagara. Following a near capture at St. David's, Willcocks and the Volunteers fight bravely at the Battle of Lundy's Lane before retreating with the American forces to within the walls of Fort Erie.

On September 4, 1814, he is killed in a skirmish setting a picket near a British Battery outside the fort.

When he died, he was the highest ranking officer in the occupying force and the Canadian Volunteers included in their officer ranks two other popularly elected members of the Upper Canadian Legislature.

Joseph Willcocks' Address to the Disaffected Mustered at Fort George, July 1813
(a little invention)

My good fellows. My true and free Canadians in exile. Many of you know me. I spoke out for your rights in The Guardian, and they silenced me. I fought for your rights in the legislature, and they called me an enemy to the King's servants. I dutifully served under Sheaffe and Brock at Queenston Heights and saw the last and only hope of true and good and free Canadians defeated by death on that fateful day in October of 1812.

I am here today to tell you that I am proud to be branded a traitor. I am flattered to be ranked among the enemies of the King's servants in the Colony. I glory in the distinction. Yes, I am the enemy of that band of sycophantic office hunters, pensioners and pimps pretending loyalty to a distant crown. I owe no allegiance to the privileged pampered sons of York. I have no duty to the transplanted Scottish shopkeep aristocracy, the wealthy, unelected, anti-democratic law makers of that doomed and rotten government.

I speak not to coerce you with threats of punishment or reprisal. I ask not for conformity, blind obedience and unquestioning acceptance of my right to command. I simply implore you as free men, free to think, free to believe, free to decide for yourself what is right, what is just, what is your duty. Will you hide like beaten dogs or will you join the war of liberation? Will you crawl under porches to lick your wounds or will you cast off your shackles and avenge yourself against those who betrayed you and stole your land? Come boys. Answer the call.

Let the world say, we risked our lives for freedom. Let the cry go up, that we made sacrifice for a true democracy of the people. That we fought for equality, fairness and justice. That we were willing to die so that our children might have a voice in their own future. Tell the world we are free men, choosing of our own free will, to take up arms against oppression. Say we dared defy the cowards and miscreants who forced us as men of conscience to flee from our homes. Let it be said that we returned to set things right.

You see I am wearing the rank of a Major, as your elected officer of choice. It is in this capacity, and with this authority, that I promise you here on this day, that when we win this war, and we will win this war, that your lands will be restored. That the neighbours who betrayed you will be punished. And that the corrupt government that drove you away will be replaced. And history will record that you were heroes. And your sons will proudly say, "My father served his country in Joe Willcock's Canadian Volunteers."

Will you fight boys? Will we give 'em hell? Let's go home like men!

"damn the Tories to hell..."

words attributed to Major Joseph Willcocks
in charge of the burning party at Newark

Burning Home

It is late December
save the plucked-white cold and dark weather
come in off the lake
where it slanted and is gone
like the drowning of storm-dead gulls
but here in Newark Niagara
cast out of these warm houses
their hearths charred with ash
enough a woman might use grey embers there
for the making of soap
the last of the old Tories
have been dragged
from their beds
to stand in shivering wet ruin
of illuminated night
for we are burning home
we are going
house by immolated house
and setting our flames
like wild bouquets
that touch their windows
for a breath of hunger wind
and the red hour
glows in fits of flicker and wilding sky
and the weeping walk away
a few old wives
and elder soldiers
wounded by their dotage
cripple off
like broken sticks
for this is *war* and the consequence of war
I'd swallow hot stones in one desire mulled

and be a hissing well
warmed and ruined by the warming
my soul sunk down
in such a heavy hole
and yet I celebrate the gravity
my spirit's found
like a falling inner darkness when we do not die
from darkness.

Treason

If you betray your neighbours
in a war.
If you burn their houses
and scour them out
into late December cold
where it is snowing
like the drifting down
of stars.
If you steal between their towns
upon a foreign horse
flaming through Saint David's
torching barns and dwellings
where old women weep
and huddle in their shawls
with flaming eyes
where water holds with fire
in one true salt.
What wise hearts
might make of this
turning madness in a furrow
with the slow and sorrow-dragged drum
of the executed and the hooded dead.
If standing on this spinning
blue-green beauty
we fly like mud from a wheel
knowing we love
and hate
this life
and yet we wonder
what it means
misunderstanding, mercy
and all the old liars

who creature the green
beneath the tumbled equilibrium
this way that way of a weathered stone.

The Lie Agreed Upon

Some would argue
that history
is an accurate and objective account of those events
of such importance as
to be noted for public record.

In this regard let us consider the case
of those residing on Canadian soil
who "betrayed" their "dutiful" allegiance to the crown of England
during the War of 1812-14
and threw their lot in
with the "invading" Americans
were variously referred to as: faint-hearted ones
      lukewarm, independent, malcontent, hostile settlers
incurably evil   fugitives

turncoats, late-come Americo-Canadians,
            suffering the taint of alienism

            traitors
        Mr. Willcocks's vile coadjutors
alien enemy   "King" Joe Willcocks's renegades

calumniators, bummers, and miscreants
vagabonds, anarchists
obnoxious and notorious characters
people of dangerous and treasonous inclination
ruffians
rebels and persons deemed suspicious characters, bad subjects,
& dangerous persons
treasonous scoundrels useless &   dissident   disaffected

                    disloyal characters
thieves, rebels, cutthroats,
villains, dissatisfied and traitorous men,
lawless rabble, mob,
marauding, violent & systematic bands of the enemy
            refugees from the Province

bad rebellious banditti
            "Americans"

did willingly participate with the multitude of traitors in "schemes" to aid the enemy in their longing for annexation and not having fear of God in his heart, nor weighing the instigation of the Devil by withdrawing the love, obedience, fidelity and allegiance owed to fellows, King and country and being armed and arrayed in a warlike and hostile manner to wit with guns, swords, and pistols, and other weapons as well offensive, did falsely, wickedly, maliciously, and traitorously in contempt of peace, the Crown, dignity and law, and to the evil example of others, willingly engage in truth of treason, misprisions of treason, and treasonable practices amounting to High Treason

the most heinous of all crimes involving

dastardly machinations, vile calumnies, having
malignant influence
through seditions
armed insurrections
predatory incursions   smash and grab raids
anarchy designed to terrorize the district

        -disorganize the militia
stealing from the needy settlers
impressing flour and grain
committing   outrages
            depredations
            degradations
            harassments
            snipings
            wanton plunderings
            barn and home burnings
making prisoners of their loyal neighbours
despoiling and harassing friends of the crown
taking revenge for private grudges
committing and perpetrating a miserable and cruel slaughter
levying war and rebellion against and within
the province of Upper Canada

giving sanctuary and
furnishing valuable information to American spies
concerning British military strength
    new fortifications, emplacements, blockhouses
    supply depots, topography, distances between communities
    state of roads, and
    best places to affect a landing for the "second" invasion

and did so carry out these actions against those referred to as:

needy settlers, former friends
neighbours
prominent and prosperous pioneers
industrious and thrifty citizens, people of loyalty, integrity,
ability,
                    trusty and well behaved
wealthy and successful residents
United Empire Loyalists
zealous loyalists
veterans of other wars
defenceless old men
mere farmers
soldiers and officers of the dutiful militia and loyal volunteers

Was there no legitimate grievance
on the part of these
self-defined foes of arbitrary power
these enemies of the King's servants?

Is it likely that they were
men of Republican ideals who resented the stranglehold
of wealth, power and property
on the part of certain
sons of privilege
and the elitists of York?

Are they victims of tyranny?
Martyrs to a cause?

Is the crime of treason
a mere matter of dates?
Is the enemy always to be defined
by an accident of borders?
Shall we revise the record?
Can any account withstand the scrutiny of strangers
to the time?
When two great wheels begin to grind
and you ask the grain
which stone it prefers to be ruined by
is it little wonder
that the grain might both cherish and resent
the irony of choice?

A Carnival of Clown's Light Now

the battle of Lundy's Lane, Niagara Falls, Canada

In the absence of this city
before her weird waxworks
gave criminal colour to the cheeks
of crime-scarred Chicago
before the brave-barrelled
lunatics rolled in the roar
at the lip of the falls
before Blondin teetered out
on a long line
balanced and breathless
above the rocks below
when old Lundy plowed these graves
and turned these birch-white bones
cannon blown in the red blast
of a gun-hot summer
when the lead shot flew thick
as crop-wreck hail
and bruised most every man flat
as pocked mud
and one soldier wrote
how the hot air
roared hoarse, loud, and strong
for hours
the musket volley vomiting death
in a dizzy drizzle
of leaden rain
and almost blinded by blood and brains
from a man shot in the head close by
in the cordite sting and squint
of smoke

followed fast in the false dark
by true dusk
and the red flower of muzzle flame
which went on and on and on
on these cruel hills
down these deadly roads
above these green waters
beneath those black heavens
upon their dead horses
into that yawning grass
from off those burning bodies
in the fat-guttering morbid light
of dead torches
in the groaning dark
after the clash of armies
went still
in this worst of wars.

The record showed that some were brave.
That the traitor Willcocks
rode a second horse
that same day because the first mount
had caught death beneath him
and shuddered onto his withers
like a butcher's bull
and that Willcocks had rallied his men
to the killing ground
and stood five hours
while the thunder doubled
and rolled its gritty stones
well into the coming of night.

And now under the grim pavement
all along the neon
flicker and Ferris wheels
and seal stunts
startle us away from true graves
while slots along the waterfront
play wheels and craps and
king-killed hands bloat
beyond the come-of-age
of bride grooms and their virgin moon
they say the gun flash
made the soldiers look
as though they laughed at dying
and two hundred years from present sorrows
when the cruel amnesias of time
have wiped us clean
come curious poets
tell us who we were
as if we'd ever cared to know.

"Oh! What are those? What is that?"

The young officer said, pointing down
at the terrors of war
while crows coughed
like sick Valkyries
those scorched angels flying in fiery thermals
like burnt paper floating above the ruined dead
and ah, their bloody scalped skulls
like gritty stones
whetted by the iron-oxide shores
of evermore.
And look you there
at the lacerated breast
where the bones break out
in a red thrill
where the heart walked deep
and drummed its blood
in a dream of mind.
What is that? though it was a man
an hour ago, once loved by a woman
in the lifelong way of wives
but what would he be
could he come to her door
without his hands
lie beside her
oozing at the eye like a squeezed rose
and what of his broken smile
his fractured kiss
his sharp touch splintered at the cuff.

And these men
made bald by the swipe of knives
knew not of the gentleness
of European wars
the musketry in enfilade
the courage of keeping the line
when they fell about
like the angry bristles of a brittle comb
seeking one true heroic darkness there
not this
solitary tumult of the soul
not this bare-skulled creature
entering the land
like the sag of graves.

Wounded By Bones

I have seen men wounded by bones
the way a cannon ball
bowls the skull clean
in a sudden blink
and splintering off of the brain
so the body falls clear
and shouldered shorter for that decollation of battle
I have stood in the smoke
in the shattering air
with the shards of an arm
like the spearing off of a snapped branch
I have seen the musket's result
in the mingling failure of reach
when the injured hand's
like a bird
flexed with a hurt in the flesh too great to fly
fluxing its phalanges
and breaking the air as it falls on its fingers
playing the earth in octaves of stone
I have seen men
lean one way
on an empty tailor's last
the long gait gone into a cruel crawl and drag
and the useless
fluttering cuff ever after pinned on a fold
while a luckless
blindness comes flinting in the shaved glass
of a femur's second use
like whittled oak.
I have seen horses dropped
screaming red graze in a green mouth.
I have stood in the storm of war

in the terrible weather of guns
and seen half men blown by on the wind
in a crimson swath of fire and blood
and felt fear rise in the gorge
sick from the heat
where the heart heaves at the throat
like a hot apple swallowed whole and hard
and we have our reasons for this
valiant romancing of noise
all mad strangers
fools to quiet dying

writer, look along your paper path
regard the ghost of silence unsullied there
and who by what hammer, by what fuse
by what flint and wick
and tear of cloth
by what spark and pan
the vanishing comes to that small touch
the unwritten whispering away of the absent hand...

From the Opposite Side of the Water

What he met
from the North Sea coast   —War
from over the English Channel   —War
from over the Irish Sea   —War
from the south shore of the lake   —War
from the east bank of the green river   —War
and then dying from war and going down
onto the dark and dreamless
ferry with his coin of purchase
the two brown pennies
of a new blindness
blinked into Charon's palm
and the calm still Styx
beneath them

From Europe to London   —War
From Dublin to York   —War
From Niagara through Black Rock
and beyond   —War
From the great capitals of four nations
War—he fell on his bones
like a shocked branch
and was gone
let us cross over the river
and rest under the shade of the trees
let us go there
let us remove from the opposite
side of the water
let us make poems from fire

let us go among wildflowers
and ditchweed
let us make from what the dead remember
garlands of forget-me-nots
let us be ordinary light
passing into a comfort of darkness.

September 4, 1814 – the present

—*part the last*—

In which much maligned and unjustly forgotten Willcocks' story res-onates forward to the struggle against Old Toryism culminating in the 1837 Rebellion, the Duncombe rebellion and the subsequent decline in power of the Family Compact.

These very same castle builders were opponents of Willcocks' dream of a free press and an effective and truly representative elected legisla-ture. These enemies of Willcocks, these old-Tory opponents of public education, land reform, and representative government with a deep and abiding hatred and distrust of the common rabble, echo down through time to our own century to remind us of ever-present concerns...

The River None Believe

I think of the Niagara
and if I say
"the river it seems remembers nothing"
and you might say
"what?" you might say "are you crazy?"
and if I say
"well, the War of 1812 was fought here
from mouth to source
and it was
the worst conflict, the most violent
ever fought by Europeans
right here on Canadian soil...
not as "remember the Alamo"
but as "remember Lundy's Lane"
the heat of battle
to the death—the worst in North America
until the Civil War
yet if you travel now
to the sight
it's like hardening of the arteries
of history
it's carnival traffic, tarmac
and the roar of a frothy falls
full of whiskey-barrel values
like empty thread spools
dangling from a mad tailor
and all you see
is Blondin on his tight rope
over the rapids
not the red wind
of a single crimson night
how many summers ago

and gone
and if I say
"go to the heights above Burlington Bay
and listen for those headless ghosts
of eight men hanged
go to Queenston
and watch the far banks
for the bad boats
go to Newark/Niagara
and look for the conflagration
listen for the hiss of torches
and the crash of blackened rafters
go to little St. David's
ride there on a dead horse
trample the vineyards
watch for the wine stain
in the blight of fire and ink"
and if by
the echo of a wet rock
if by the strangled cry
of some turning eddy
foaming round in eternal rubble
wearing the shape of the flow
perilous enough
to the jarred heel
to spin a man's craft
and crack his memory loose
as quick as a war club will
and if I look
to this land
and see
how a man is missed
as if he were never there
how his shape might drop away
like a walker in the fog

some phantom colour fading in the mist
with a ragged twin
of someone watching from the other way
what of this
this earth that holds us
this deeper gravity

this float of stones

these stories
dead tongues tell?

Martyrs in the Landscape

for James Reaney

My body's beneath pavement
in the shadow of the grey bridge
under the drunken
parking lot across from Buffalo, Black Rock
and beyond, I am down beneath where veterans stagger out
shaking their keys
to find their locks
in the whiskey blur of dusk
my bones like roots
of trees no longer there
among the other anonymous dead
no more the British battery, unheard
no more the lethal thunder
—this, the feckless cannonade
of over-wearied light
the moon-slow lob of night
broken upon the blue wall
of dawn again
and still beneath the hum of rigs
that buzz like bug storms
above the green Niagara's beery foam.
Take your shovel to the tarmac
break the gummy gravel
to a grave
and let me breathe
who breathes no more
let me haunt the windy shadows
like the ash
of fire buried not quite out

let every embered step
bestir a hundred smothered voices
like horses coming home
the rapids at a river's turn
the visions of a crooked lane gone blind beyond a curve

of all discouraged corpses
in a mob of bones
disappearing backwards
from this dishonoured day
my silence, like the moody curses
of unloved men
my quiet, like a groaning barn.

Waterless Children

Drawing from these
deep old Tory wells

—Ontario—

we call upon
circumference and circumstance
made most compact
and to an ancient villainy recalled
we drop the empty bucket down

and listen

while a hollow heart resounds.

Notes on the poems

Dead Angels Bless Us All:
Willcocks being born the second son of Anglo-Irish gentry, had no hope of inheritance or property

The River Liffey Near Dublin:
born at "the Mills," Palmerston, on the banks of the River Liffey four kilometers west of Dublin, Joseph was raised as a sporting youth who loved to fish and hunt and ramble with his dog in an idyllic setting described in contemporary accounts as one of the most beautiful in all of Europe

The Fever of Stolen Property:
the women of the 18th century were often quite sporting and they wore beauty spots to signify their love lives. A spot on the forehead tells perspective suitors that they are free-loving. Willcocks enjoyed the company of lovely women, but swore he would marry only a woman of means preferring the pleasures of older women with prospects and property

Excellent Reasons to Hate:
the rebellion of 1798 was quite violent and it swirled around the Willcocks' residence and had a very deleterious impact upon the fortunes of Joseph's father. Although rumours that he participated in the rebellion or at the very least had sympathies with the rebel cause plagued Joseph and are even given some credence by historians, it is very clear that these rumours are completely false and without foundation

Exile:
Joseph left Ireland because he had no prospects at home, and indeed would have ruined his family if he had stayed. He emigrated to Upper Canada drawn there by the promise of land from his distant cousin William Willcocks

What of These Names:
Society at York was fraught with pretension and conflict. The names listed in this poem are simply some of those of "high society" living in York at the time of Willcocks' arrival

If I Dared to Dream of Father Dying:
Joseph wrote home quite frequently in the first few years after his arrival at York, addressing many of his letters to his father who had died shortly after Joseph left for Upper Canada. When Joseph finally hears the news of his father's death, he reveals that he saw his father in a dream around the time he had died

The Portrait Not Quite There:
although Joseph's cousins William Willcocks and Peter Russell's portraits were painted, his image was never set down, nor are there extant descriptions of his appearance though it seems clear from his life with the ladies that he was not unattractive. The portraits of many of York society, including those of William Willcocks and Peter Russell were painted by William Berczy (b. Johann Albert Ulrich Moll) painter, architect, colonizer, who along with his son William was a frequent dinner guest at the home of Joseph Willcocks

Reading Circle:
while in residence at the Russell home, Joseph spent most evenings either playing whist or listening to Peter Russell read from works of literature. Russell was quite vain and proud of the quality of his reading voice. Willcocks who was a very active young man soon became bored with the sedentary sameness of life in York

My Heart is Wrung:
Joseph's best friend and sometime drinking companion, the politically radical and slightly erratic lawyer William Weekes, was killed by his law partner in a duel

Writing When the Ink is Cold:
Joseph kept a diary and copies of all his letters. He was Peter Russell's personal secretary and eventually became a journalist and politician. His Diary and Letter Book is the property of the National Archives in

Ottawa and extant copies of his newspaper, "The Upper Canadian Guardian or Freeman's Journal" are held in London, England

When You Throw a Man in the Lake:
Joseph was hot tempered and loose tongued. He threw a servant in the lake for carelessly tethering his boat

Caught Pulling the Cord Together:
Joseph was dismissed by his employer, Peter Russell, for daring to presume to court Russell's sister, Elizabeth

A Disapproval of Stones:
Joseph managed Russell's farm and then the property of Chief Justice Allcocks. His last diary entry reveals a visit to the property and the discovery of stones on the land. His closing words were "we did not approve"

Debts:
Joseph left Ireland deeply in debt. Soon after his arrival in Upper Canada he sent money home to settle his affairs. Shortly after his arrival in Upper Canada he witnessed the hanging of an Irishman convicted of the crime of forgery

Watching the Wolves:
Joseph managed several farms over the years and after he was elected to parliament, one of his principle concerns was the presence of wolves in the community and their predatory theft of livestock

The Age of Reason:
the span of Willcocks' life occurred during what has come to be referred to by historians as "the age of reason" it was also an age of revolution and war

Ill Emissary:
Joseph Willcocks was invited to dine with Brock and presented with the assignment of travelling to the Grand River Natives as his emissary in the hopes of persuading the Natives to throw their lot in with the British in the War. The Natives had been approached by the Americans who wished them to stay neutral, which was their inclination. And Indian Agent Claus

was an enemy of Willcocks. Claus stood accused of corruption and bribery, was despised by most of the Native chiefs, and had accused Willcocks of sedition earlier that year. Willcocks, despite personal illness, travelled to the Grand and spoke with the Chiefs. A letter stating his account of that meeting was sent to Brock's adjutant, Macdonell. Willcocks succeeded in his mission. However, historians seemed quite perplexed at Brock's judgement, and some even called into question whether this Willcocks was the same man as the one who turned traitor the following summer

Gentleman Volunteer:
Willcocks served with distinction on the side of the British under General Sheaffe in the Battle of Queenston Heights. Sheaffe arrived to win the day shortly after General Brock had died in battle

Before the Parliament Was Burned:
the parliament of York was burned by the invading Americans in April 1813. The parliament buildings had served as a church as well as a legislature. Willcocks diaries mention the Sunday sermons and he was a popularly elected representative for the riding of York, Haldimand and Lincoln for three successive terms beginning with his first term in 1808

Joseph Willcocks' Address to the Disaffected:
In July of 1813, Joseph crossed over to the other side at Fort George and offered his services to the enemy, raising a force of disaffected Canadians calling themselves the "Canadian Volunteers." Willcocks was elected Major and then promoted to the rank of Lieutenant Colonel

Burning Home:
in late December of 1813, on the orders of American General McClure, Willcocks led a burning party which torched the town of Newark (formerly Niagara, now Niagara-on-the-Lake) before the retreating army went back across the border

Treason:
Joseph Willcocks was convicted of the crime of High Treason in absentia at the Ancaster Assizes in May of 1814. Eight of the men convicted in that trial were hanged-drawn-and-quartered at Burlington Heights on July 20, 1814

The Lie Agreed Upon:
the words of this piece are taken from historical texts

A Carnival of Clown's Light Now:
Joseph Willcocks participated at the Battle of Lundy's Lane in July 1814, rallying his volunteers on several occasions and having a horse shot out from under him. This battle is the most intense and devastating battle ever fought on Canadian soil

Oh! What are those? What is that?:
the title of this poem is a direct quotation from a young officer upon seeing the mutilated corpse of a scalped soldier

The River None Believe:
most of the battle sites of the war of 1812 are paved over and lost to the modern world. This is especially true of the site of the Battle of Lundy's Lane, where the most violent struggle in Canadian history was fought . . . the Niagara district suffered the worst and most continuous fighting of the brief two-year war, having been occupied by a large American force in both late 1813 and for most of the summer of 1814 . . . the towns of Newark and St. David's were burned and the American side of the water suffered much the same with the burning of Buffalo, Black Rock and beyond

Afterward:
A Matter of Treason — The Life and Times of Joseph Willcocks
1773 – September 4, 1814

I sit in the parking lot of the Legion in Fort Erie, Ontario. Here, the world that was, is paved over, hemmed in, lost in the rig-drone of the city under the long grey shadow of the Peace Bridge connecting Canada to industrial Buffalo. The green Niagara seems but a slow thought flowing by. I've come to contemplate a death, unmourned. Unfound bones. Somewhere beneath me, in among the multitude of anonymous dead, lie the unshriven remains of one who fell so long ago he's dust. And what I feel is the great disappointment of absent ghosts. The busy indifference of truckers and tourists. Amnesia of asphalt, black and smelling of tar, impervious to light, opaque and unforgiving. Here I sit, where the veterans of the last great war come to remember and forget, to revere and regret, to honour heroes and grieve the dead, to say of their fellows, "I knew him once, he was my friend," and to weep at the thought of him gone, and to laugh for the days spent together when they were all young.

I try to think of the rain and smoke and heat and long-ago noise of a different battle. I try to think, here, on this very ground, was the British battery set to lay siege on old Fort Erie, 800 yards away. One man leading a smallish band of men, came in wet September, proud in his officer's uniform, brave in his mission, setting a picket to keep America on this hard won place. How many waters had he crossed since youth? How many friends betrayed on the way? How many trusts dishonoured? How many loves disappointed? And what were his thoughts when he fell, for a cheer went up in the ranks when he died, though some of those close lost heart. And when he was found by his foe, next day, they were thrilled he was gone, and they threw his cold corpse in the ground, and shovelled the earth on his face which was dead to the light.

Only the day before his neighbour had taken aim and brought him down with one musket ball hot to the right breast so his lungs bubbled blood and he drowned in his own red breath. Only the rain-dark day before. And it was his last afternoon, the one on which the supper hour never came for him. Around four p.m., on September 4th, 1814, he lost the last of light. Exactly here, where I sit now, in the rushing by of cars, in this distracted hour, I conjure something of the smoke of what he was from the fumes of the here and now.

And no one, it seems, is more alone in the world, than a traitor found, but a traitor dead is less than a stone. And what his eyes could see, his tongue taste, his hands grasp, were all gone as in a poor and dreamless sleep. I hold in memory, the large loop of his clear cursive, his legible letters full of hope and care, his diaries marking his days among friends. And I think as well of the cane he carried, lost in a closet somewhere in the world, because he gave it away while he lived. And the man who shared his initials, touched down through time until the story wore away, and the cane became forgetful as any other stick let fall by a tree struck dead. And whoever walks out the door, leans on that ghost's wood unaware that someone once loved his company and called him friend. And if there's nothing left of the Irish boy who grieved the news of the death of his father at home across the ocean, if nothing remains of the brother betrayed by his blood when he found himself refused by his own, if there's nothing left of the broken-hearted suitor snubbed by the lady for his lack of station in life, if there's nothing left of the drinker's joy, and the wild and sportive youth, if there's nothing left of grief at the loss of his best friend in a duel, if there's nothing left of the past in the noise of this day, then why are we ever alive?

Born at "the Mills," on the Liffey four miles west of Dublin, Ireland, in 1773, Joseph was the second son of Robert Willcocks and Jane Willcocks (nee Powell). Their religion was Church of Ireland, and though their fortunes were in serious decline, Robert remained a man of some local prominence, and Joseph's older brother, Richard, went on to be knighted by the crown and some claim Richard as father of modern policing.

By the time of his departure from Ireland in December 1799 as a twenty-eight-year-old scion of a family in serious financial crisis, he had accumulated personal debts which he had no hope of settling, unless he departed. Being a "second son" and having no prospects at home, referring to himself as a "distressed person," he turned his sights upon Canada.

Encouraged to emigrate by his distant cousin, William Willcocks, leaving behind an elderly and ailing father, a beloved mother, two siblings (Richard and Lucy) and an idyllic setting on the Liffey, Joseph set sail December 1, 1799 from the west wall in Dublin for the new world aboard the ship, *The Fortune*.

The voyage was very much beset by storm, and after a passage of nearly seventy-four days, he arrived at New York, on February 12, 1800. After a brief stay in New York state, he arrived at York on March 20, 1800. Though he discovered that William had little to offer him, Joseph was able to acquire employment as the personal secretary to another relative, his distant cousin, Peter Russell, who was then the most powerful man residing in Upper Canada.

He moved in with the Russells and managed Peter's affairs for close to two years. During that time he acquired lease to 1,200 acres of land near Whitby and a town lot in York. His rise in society was hampered by false rumour that he had participated in the Rebellion of 1798 in Ireland. Within two short years after his arrival, he alienated his employers affections by presuming to court Russell's sister and found himself with neither position nor accommodation.

Fortunately, Chief Justice Allcock took Joseph's part, hired him and gave him shelter in his own home. By 1804, within the sphere of Allcock's influence, Joseph was appointed Sheriff of the Home District and by the following year was living in his own house with a man-servant.

However, with the departure of Allcock and the arrival of Judge Thorpe, Joseph's life took a significant turn. York resident John

Richardson, who had known Joseph for some time, perceived "a great alteration in the conduct of Willcocks towards the end of 1805." And Willcocks soon found himself at loggerheads with Lieutenant-Governor Gore, who had him removed from the office of Sheriff as of April 23, 1807.

At that point Joseph left Upper Canada for New York State, travelling there with the express purpose of purchasing a printing press and establishing a political newspaper. Although Gore suspected Willcocks of plotting to overthrow the government of Upper Canada, there was no evidence to prove his suspicions.

By July, 1807 Joseph Willcocks had returned to Newark, and in that month he began publishing the *Upper Canadian Guardian or Freeman's Journal.* In addition to publishing his radical newspaper, he ran for election to the Legislative Assembly in January 1808 and was popularly voted in as representative for the riding of West York, Lincoln, and Haldimand.

Although he argued in favour of representative democracy, public education and agricultural reform, Willcocks found himself charged with libel, slander and language highly derogatory to the dignity of the House. On one occasion, he was found guilty and was committed to jail where he remained for more than a month in conditions described as "not fit for a pig." His committal is characterized in a newspaper account of the day: "all casual accounts agree that Mr. Willcocks is most cruelly and unjustly treated."

On June 18, 1812 the United States declared war on England. In August of that year, General Brock asked Joseph Willcocks to dine with him. He appointed Willcocks the task of travelling to the Grand River Natives to persuade them to join the British cause in the War. Though quite ill, Willcocks performed his duty and sent a letter to that effect dated September 1, 1812 addressing his remarks to Brock's adjutant, John Macdonell.

In October 1812, Willcocks served as a gentleman volunteer with bravery and distinction under the leadership of General Sheaffe at the Battle of Queenston Heights. The following February, in the second session of the 6th Parliament, Willcocks is referred to as a "zealous loyalist." As of April, 1813, he was actively involved in the recruitment of local militia. William Hamilton Merritt said of him, "he has behaved very well on all occasions and so have all his party." Merritt added, "although they are trusted with no office whatsoever."

Then in late July of 1813, Willcocks abandoned the British cause and went over to the Americans occupying Fort George. He offered his services to the enemy, and on July 10, was authorized to raise a force of disaffected Canadians to fight under the American flag. He was elected major of the force which he called *The Canadian Volunteers*.

As of July 17, 1813, Major Joseph Willcocks corps of Canadian Volunteers consisted of eight officers and forty-four rank and file. They were outfitted by the United States but received no pay. They were distinguished in dress by a white cockade and a green ribbon in their hats. They served as guides for the army that summer, recruiting one hundred and thirty disaffected Canadians by September. Willcocks was praised for his "activity and bravery."

During the autumn of 1813, their nighttime raids yielded information and plundered supplies. Their principle opponent was Captain William Hamilton Merritt. The conflict between these two adversaries plagued the Niagara District for the remainder of the year with little benefit to either side. Willcocks' men even went so far as to take captive Merritt's own father. Merritt began to refer to Willcocks disparagingly as "King Joe." By November, two other members of the Legislative Assembly joined the Canadian Volunteers. Benajah Mallory and Abraham Markle had been relatively constant supporters of the loose opposition, which Lieutenant-Governor Gore had called "Joe's party." Willcocks, promoted to Lieutenant-Colonel, appointed Mallory a major, and Markle a captain.

At 5 p.m. on December 10, in the cold of winter, with the impending retreat of the Americans from Upper Canada at Fort George, Brigadier-General McClure issued an order to burn the village of Newark. Willcocks and his followers turned the occupants out into the cold winter snows and torched the town of which Willcocks had been a resident for six years.

Shortly thereafter, Willcocks travelled to Washington for an audience with American Secretary of War, John Armstrong. Having met with

Armstrong in February, he returned to the Canadian Volunteers having succeeded in gaining official recognition of his force. Armstrong granted Willcocks and his officers commissions as officers of volunteers in the service of the United States. Willcocks returned to the Niagara frontier and resumed his command May 1, 1814.

That same month, Willcocks, Mallory and Markle were convicted in absentia of High Treason at the Ancaster Assize. At Burlington Heights on July 20, eight men were hanged-drawn-and-quartered, thus making consequences of capture abundantly clear. Seven days prior to the execution, American General Brown had invaded Upper Canada at Fort Erie. During the following weeks, Willcocks served mostly as a guide for the invaders. On July 17, he narrowly escaped capture near the village of St. David's. On July 25 at the Battle of Lundy's Lane, Willcocks fought heroically, rallying his men on several occasions in the heat of battle, at one point having had his horse shot out from under him.

After the Battle of Lundy's Lane, the Americans withdrew to within the walls of Fort Erie. On August 16, Willcocks assumed temporary command of the brigade stationed there, thus becoming the highest ranking officer in the American army then occupying Upper Canada.

On September 4, 1814, forty-one-year-old Joseph Willcocks died from a fatal wound in the right breast. He fell somewhere between four and five in the afternoon while setting a picket near the British Battery located in the woods eight hundred yards outside the earthworks of Fort Erie. His passing was mourned by fellow officer Matteson with these words "his undaunted valour had acquired the entire confidence of officers and soldiers . . . of Colonel Willcocks, I take pleasure in announcing that in every movement he behaved as a hero and patriot. Calm and unruffled, he rushed on in defense of our country's rights until he fell entwined with the laurels of glory..."

So why would this former Sheriff of the Home District, this elected representative of the Upper Canadian Legislative Assembly, this publisher of our first political newspaper, this courageous gentleman volunteer, this one-time emissary for General Brock, this scion of a gentrified Anglo-Irish family, cross over to the enemy in the middle of the War of 1812?

The timing of Willcocks' defection might in part be explained by the appointment as leader of the British forces in Upper Canada of Major General de Rottenburg. De Rottenburg arrived to take up his command at the Head-of-the-Lake (Burlington Bay) on June 29th, 1813. Willcocks offered his services to American General Dearborn at Fort George on July 10th, two days after de Rottenburg's first skirmish there on July 8th. It has been written of de Rottenburg that he seemed quite prepared to withdraw regular forces and abandon much of the territory of western Upper Canada.

The proroguing of parliament had given a free hand to the Tory elite of the Upper House who were clamouring for an imposition of martial law and the suspension of habeas corpus. De Rottenburg had previously imposed martial law in eastern Upper Canada. Willcocks had already experienced the consequences of martial law in his beloved Ireland. He had also experienced incarceration without trial at York. With power in the hands of the appointed Upper House, many loyal Canadians were already being seized and jailed without trial. Confirmation of the connection between Willcocks' defection and his thoughts of Ireland might be found in the name chosen for the force of disaffected Canadians. "Canadian Volunteers" echoes the name, "Irish Volunteers," which had been the name for the Whig supporters of an Irish Parliament in Ireland. Willcocks' newspaper had taken its name from the Whig press in Dublin, "The Freeman's Journal."

Charles Beardsley, son of lawyer Bartholomew Beardsley of Newark, published a novel at Buffalo in 1847 in an effort to answer that very question. His novel, *Victims of Tyranny*, has as its central character, a Sheriff Joseph Willcocks. The fictional story line roughly parallels that of the real Willcocks. Ironically Beardsley's father had been one of the lawyers representing the men charged with high treason at the Ancaster Assizes. Beardsley senior was hounded out of the district, and upon his death was remembered as a man of fine judgement who "had some peculiar ideas which were too advanced for his time."

Political dissident Robert Gourlay would write of Willcocks in 1818: "after Queenston, he could obtain neither favour nor mercy from the provincial government. At last, starving and exasperated he deserted to the enemy—after doing his devoirs like a man at the Battle of Queenston Heights. Even this obtained for him neither complaisance nor immunity from abuse. He found himself ruined in fortune, opposed and hated by those in authority, without any prospect before him but starvation...in a moment of exasperation he deserted the ranks."

That he was beloved in the memory of many is unequivocal. Jonathan Woolverton, an innkeeper at Grimsby, remembered him fondly and for all his later years carried Willcocks' silver-headed cane bearing the initials they shared, J.W.. And he treasured Willcocks' personal diaries and letters, bequeathing them by way of his great-grandson to the Canadian National Archives. According to the editor's preface to the published diaries, they give us a "closer knowledge of the manners of domestic life than can be found anywhere else." This same editor writes of Joseph saying he is "plainly a gentleman, well-educated, intelligent, truthful, capable and courageous."

Joseph Willcocks, vilified traitor, second son of Robert Willcocks and Mary Powell of *The Mills* on the Liffey, Palmerston, Ireland, rests beneath the pavement in an unmarked grave at Fort Erie, Ontario in the shadow of the Peace Bridge. Let us then honour the dead. Let us defy the great simplifiers. Let us rescue even complicated stories from silence. Let us bring his face to the light.

"It is the author's conclusion that Joseph Willcocks' sole reason for forming the Canadian Volunteers was to further his own personal and political ambitions."
Donald E. Graves, M.A. Thesis, 1982

*"To find a consistent and rational thread in Willcocks'
political career it is not necessary to discount his words
and emphasize his treason; rather, it may be found in
paying closer attention to what he said, when he said
it, what he did, and when he did it. Firmly in the oppo-
sition Whig tradition, Willcocks opposed arbitrary and
distant power, valued loyalty to his country rather than
to his rulers, and believed in the independence of colonial
legislatures. At great inconvenience to his own position,
he pursued a public course consistent with those Whig
principles."*

Elwood H. James, "Joseph Willcocks,"
Dictionary of Canadian Biography

Internationally acclaimed author John B. Lee has published thirty books to date and is the recipient of numerous international awards. In 1995 he won the Tilden Award (C.B.C./Saturday Night Magazine) and he is the only two time winner of the Milton Acorn Memorial People's Poetry Award. He lives and writes in Brantford, Ontario.